My Scripture Workbook

BIBLE VERSES ABOUT

Character

this book belongs to:

ALLISON Chevelle Kauffman

Dear Parents,

Thank you for choosing this resource! All Scripture is breathed out by God and is the source of divine, absolute authority (2 Timothy 3:16-17). His Word is necessary for us to be complete and equipped for every good work He has prepared in advance for us to do. It is sufficient for all of our needs—it comforts, convicts, and nourishes us to grow in godliness (John 17:17). It is also the weapon by which we can overcome the desires of our flesh and the assaults of the enemy (Ephesians 6:17).

Therefore, teaching the Word to our children is a worthy investment of time and energy. We are responsible for guarding their children's minds, and they should endeavor to fill them with God's Word. This can be done in many ways—engagement in a local church, intentional conversations, direct recitation of verses, an audio Bible, family devotionals, and transcription.

Transcription is a championed practice for children for many reasons. It improves penmanship, advances spelling skills, and presents proper sentence structures, but more importantly, it is a powerful aid in memorization. It encourages children to slow down and employ many of their senses to engage the text at hand. It also provides the opportunity to dig deeper into a memory verse by providing the time and space for discussion between the parent and the child.

My Scripture Workbook is a tool for parents to help their children hide God's Word in their hearts. Parents are given more focused time with the child to discuss the passage. As a child transcribes the verse on the dotted lines, it will aid in the storage of the Scripture in his or her mind. This is one tool to equip our children with strategies to memorize, which are skills that will last a lifetime and greatly enhance their ability to hide God's Word in their minds and hearts.

Helpful Tips

- The workbook can be completed at any pace, but a mastery approach is recommended.

- The child can begin the journey of memorization by reading the verse out loud and then transcribing it in the workbook. They can then read it aloud a few more times.

- The following day, the parent and child can approach the same verse in a different way. Some options could be creating hand motions or drawing a picture to represent the verse. Perhaps they can create a rhythm by clapping their hands as they read the verse, allowing the simple cadence to cement the verse in their minds.

- The workbook provides ease of reviewing prior verses. Mastered memory work often requires periodic review.

- The character trait can be the basis for character training on top of memory work. The workbook provides a common working ground for the parent and child.

Table of Contents by Topic

Boldness	39, 45, 79
Compassion	5, 15
Contentment	63
Creativity	97
Deference	75
Determination	65, 95
Devotion	55, 87, 93
Diligence	13
Discernment	27
Endurance	9
Enthusiasm	19
Faith	33, 53
Forgiveness	91
The Fruit of the Spirit	7
Generosity	59, 85
Hospitality	61
Humility	11, 21, 49
Initiative	25
Joyfulness	83, 101
Love	51, 99
Meekness	67, 71, 77
Obedience	17, 37, 47, 73
Reverence	35
Thankfulness	29, 43, 81
Truthfulness	69
Trust	89, 103
Virtue	23, 33, 57
Wisdom	41

Let's write about

Compassion

Use the lines on the next page to copy today's Bible verse!

And be kind and compassionate to one another, forgiving one another, just as God also forgave you in Christ.

Ephesians 4:32

First, write your name: Allison Chevelle Kauffman

And be kind and compassionate to one another, forgiving one another, Just as God also forgave you in christ

Ephesians 4:32

Let's write about
the Fruit of the Spirit

Use the lines on the next page to copy today's Bible verse!

But the fruit of the Spirit is love, joy, peace, patience, kindness, goodness, faithfulness, gentleness, and self-control. The law is not against such things

Galatians 5:22-23

First, write your name: Allison Chevelle Kauffman

but the fruit of the spirit is love, joy, peace, patience, kindness, goodness and self-control. The law is not against such things Galatians 5:22-23

Let's write about
Endurance

Use the lines on the next page to copy today's Bible verse!

Blessed is the one who endures trials, because when he has stood the test he will receive the crown of life that God has promised to those who love him.

James 1:12

First, write your name: Allison

Blessed is the One who endures Trials, because when he has stood the Test he will receive the crown of life that God has promised to those who love him

James 1:12

Let's write about
Humility

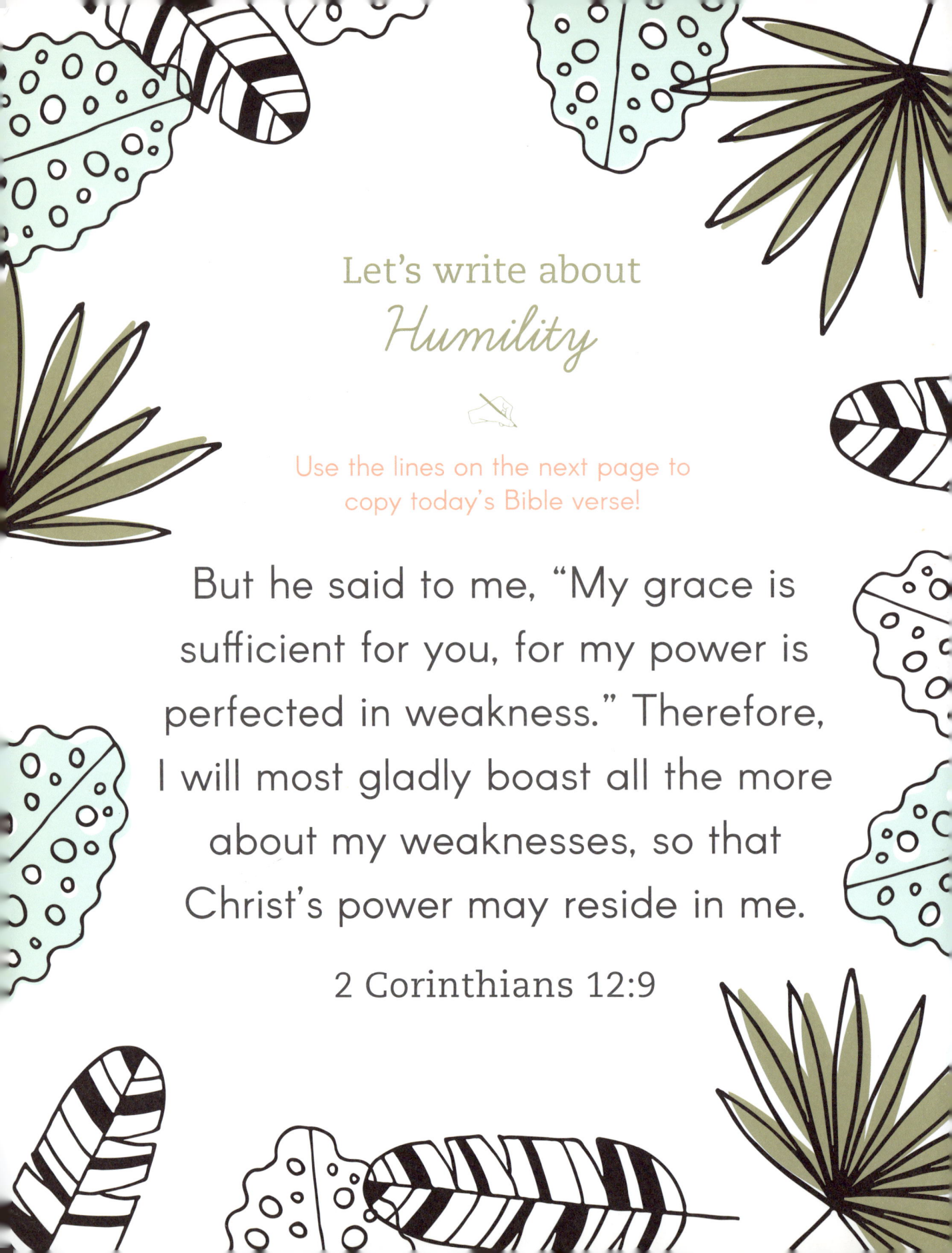

Use the lines on the next page to copy today's Bible verse!

But he said to me, "My grace is sufficient for you, for my power is perfected in weakness." Therefore, I will most gladly boast all the more about my weaknesses, so that Christ's power may reside in me.

2 Corinthians 12:9

First, write your name: Allison

But he said to me My grace is sufficient for you, for my power is perfect is weakness. Therefore, I will most gladly boast all the more about my weaknesses, so that Christ's power may reside in me

2 CORINTHIAS 12:9

Let's write about

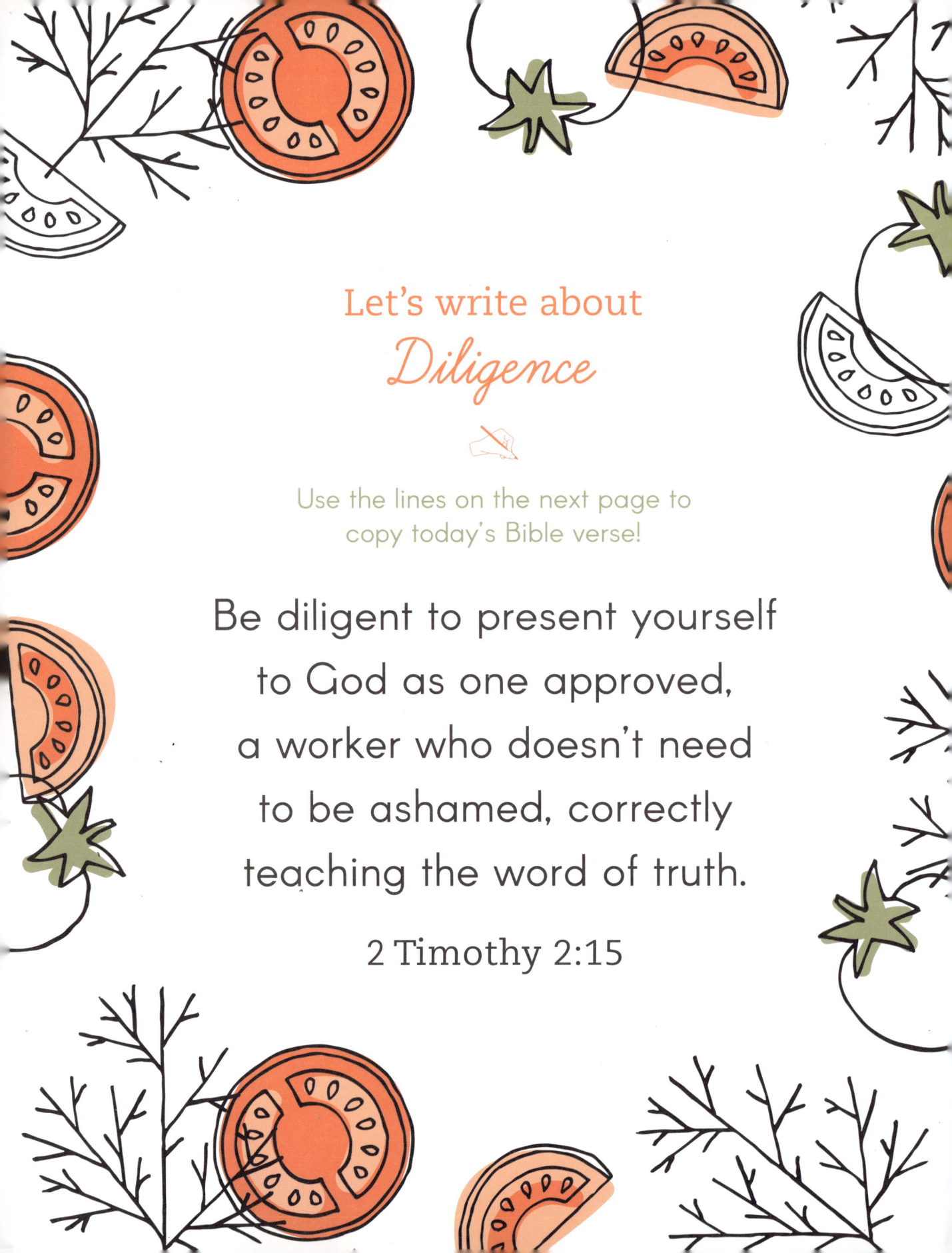

Diligence

Use the lines on the next page to copy today's Bible verse!

Be diligent to present yourself to God as one approved, a worker who doesn't need to be ashamed, correctly teaching the word of truth.

2 Timothy 2:15

First, write your name: Allison

Be diligent to present yourself to God as one approved a worker who dosen't need to be ashamed, correctly teaching the word of truth

2 Timothy 2:15

Let's write about

Compassion

Use the lines on the next page to copy today's Bible verse!

But I say to you who listen: Love your enemies, do what is good to those who hate you,

Luke 6:27

First, write your name: Allison

But I say to you who listen: Love your enemies, do what is good to those who hate you,

Luke 6:27

Let's write about
Obedience

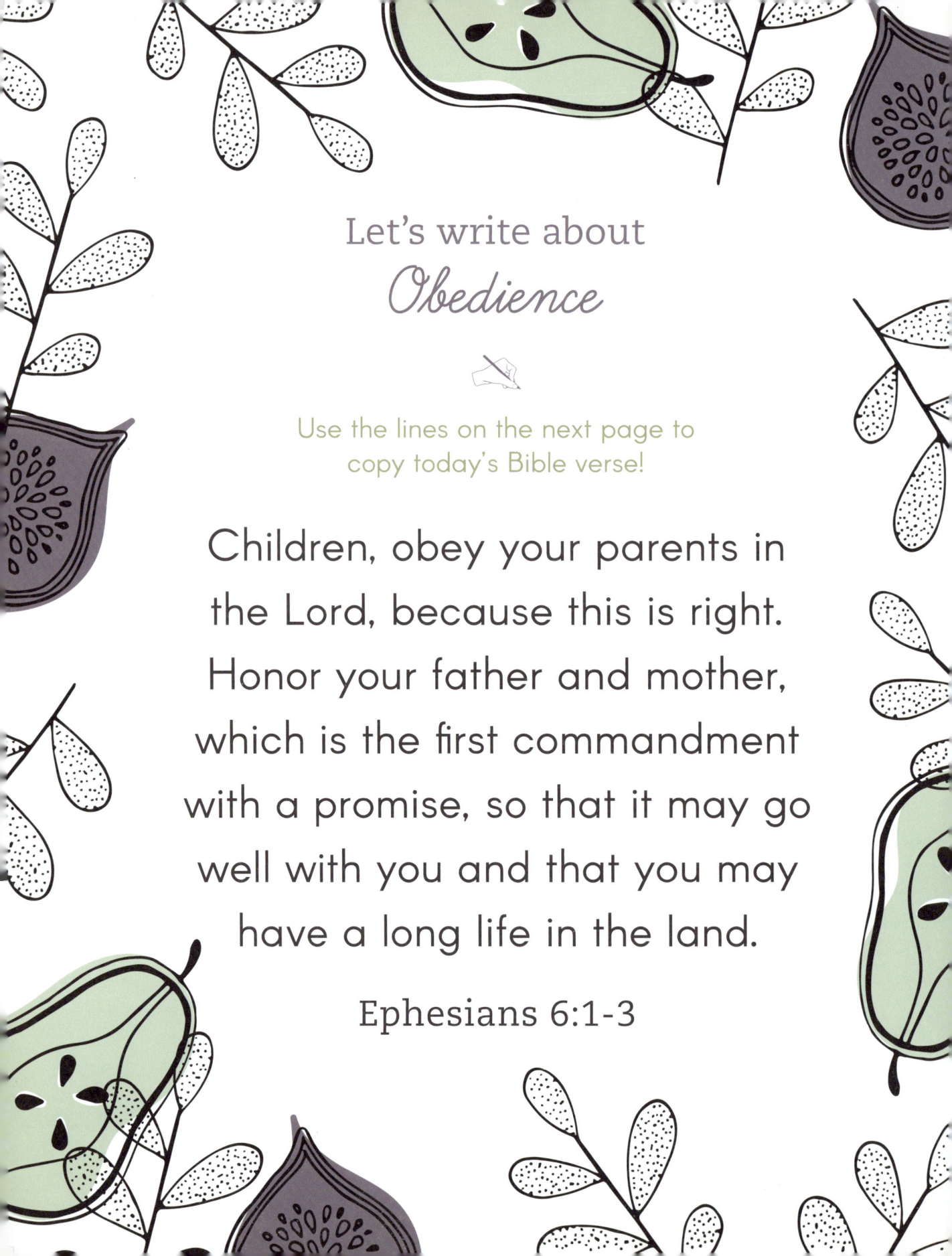

Use the lines on the next page to copy today's Bible verse!

Children, obey your parents in the Lord, because this is right. Honor your father and mother, which is the first commandment with a promise, so that it may go well with you and that you may have a long life in the land.

Ephesians 6:1-3

First, write your name: ALLISON

Children obey your parents in the Lord, because this is rilght. Honer you father and mother, wich is the first commandment

Let's write about
Enthusiasm

Use the lines on the next page to copy today's Bible verse!

Do everything without grumbling and arguing, so that you may be blameless and pure, children of God who are faultless in a crooked and perverted generation, among whom you shine like stars in the world.

Philippians 2:14-15

First, write your name: Allison

Do everything without grumbling and arguing, so that you may be blameless and pure, children of God who are faultless in a crooked and perverted generation, among whom you shine like stars in the world. philippians 2:14-15

Let's write about
Humility

Use the lines on the next page to copy today's Bible verse!

Do nothing out of selfish ambition or conceit, but in humility consider others as more important than yourselves.

Philippians 2:3

First, write your name: Allison

Do nothing out of selfish ambition or conceit but

Let's write about

Virtue

Use the lines on the next page to copy today's Bible verse!

Do not love the world or the things in the world. If anyone loves the world, the love of the Father is not in him.

1 John 2:15

First, write your name: a b c d e f

g h i j k l m n o p q

r s

q r s t u v
w x y z

Let's write about
Initiative

Use the lines on the next page to copy today's Bible verse!

Don't let anyone despise your youth, but set an example for the believers in speech, in conduct, in love, in faith, and in purity.

1 Timothy 4:12

First, write your name

Let's write about

Discernment

Use the lines on the next page to copy today's Bible verse!

Do not be conformed to this age, but be transformed by the renewing of your mind, so that you may discern what is the good, pleasing, and perfect will of God.

Romans 12:2

First, write your name

Let's write about
Thankfulness

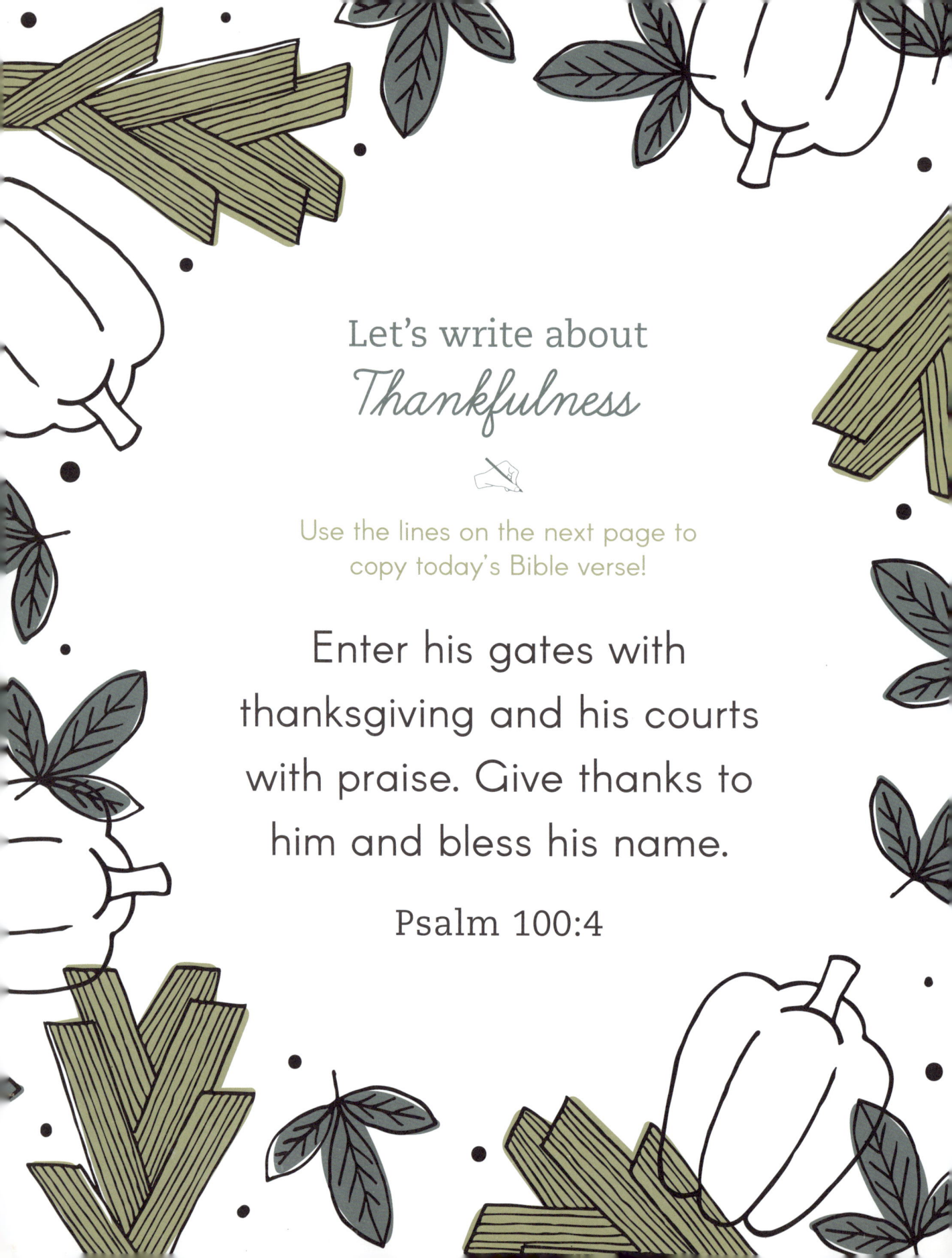

Use the lines on the next page to copy today's Bible verse!

Enter his gates with thanksgiving and his courts with praise. Give thanks to him and bless his name.

Psalm 100:4

First, write your name

Let's write about
Virtue

Use the lines on the next page to
copy today's Bible verse!

Finally brothers and sisters, whatever is true, whatever is honorable, whatever is just, whatever is pure, whatever is lovely, whatever is commendable—if there is any moral excellence and if there is anything praiseworthy—dwell on these things.

Philippians 4:8

First, write your name

Let's write about
Faith

Use the lines on the next page to copy today's Bible verse!

For our momentary light affliction is producing for us an absolutely incomparable eternal weight of glory. So we do not focus on what is seen, but on what is unseen. For what is seen is temporary, but what is unseen is eternal.

2 Corinthians 4:17-18

First, write your name

Let's write about
Reverence

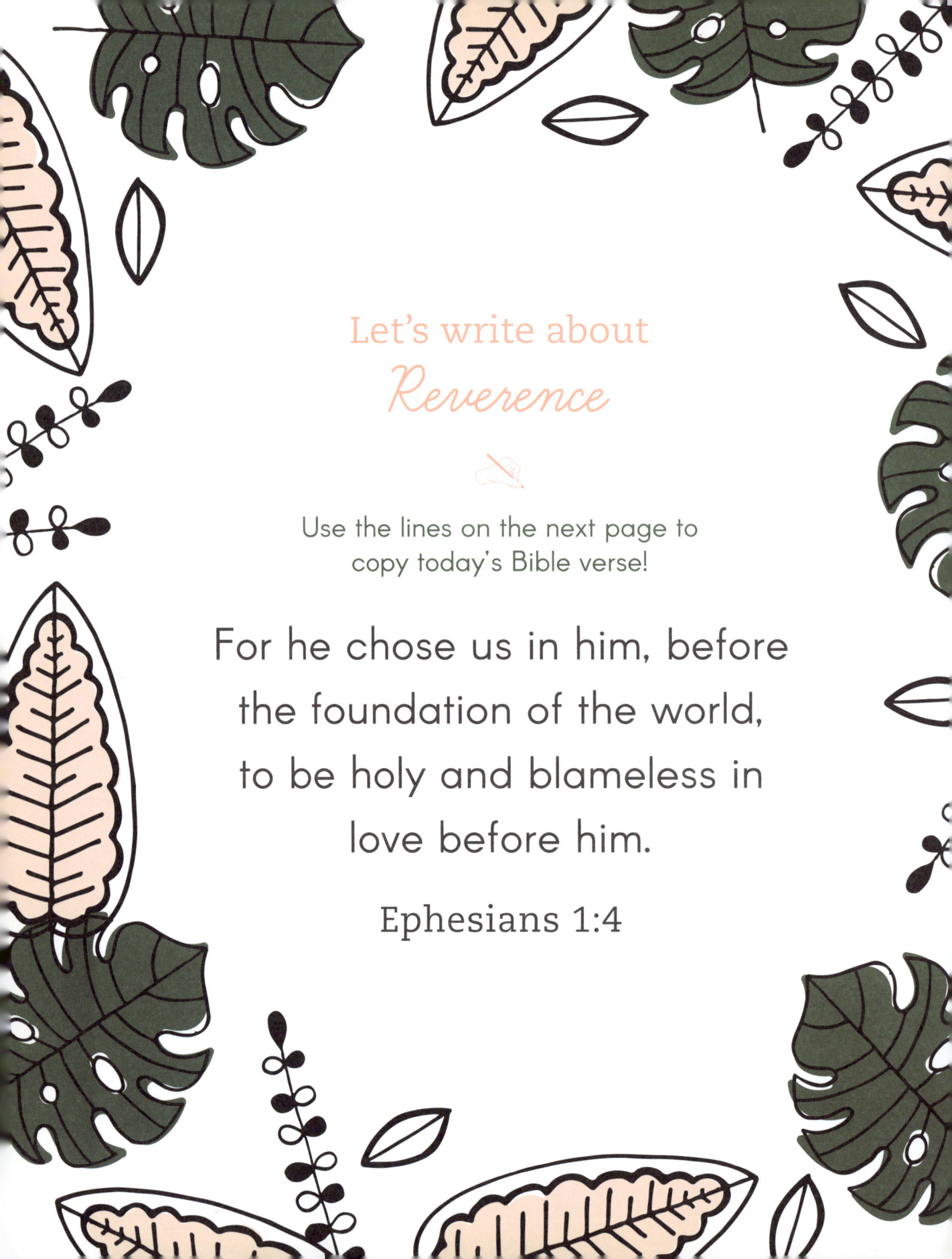

Use the lines on the next page to copy today's Bible verse!

For he chose us in him, before the foundation of the world, to be holy and blameless in love before him.

Ephesians 1:4

First, write your name

Let's write about
Obedience

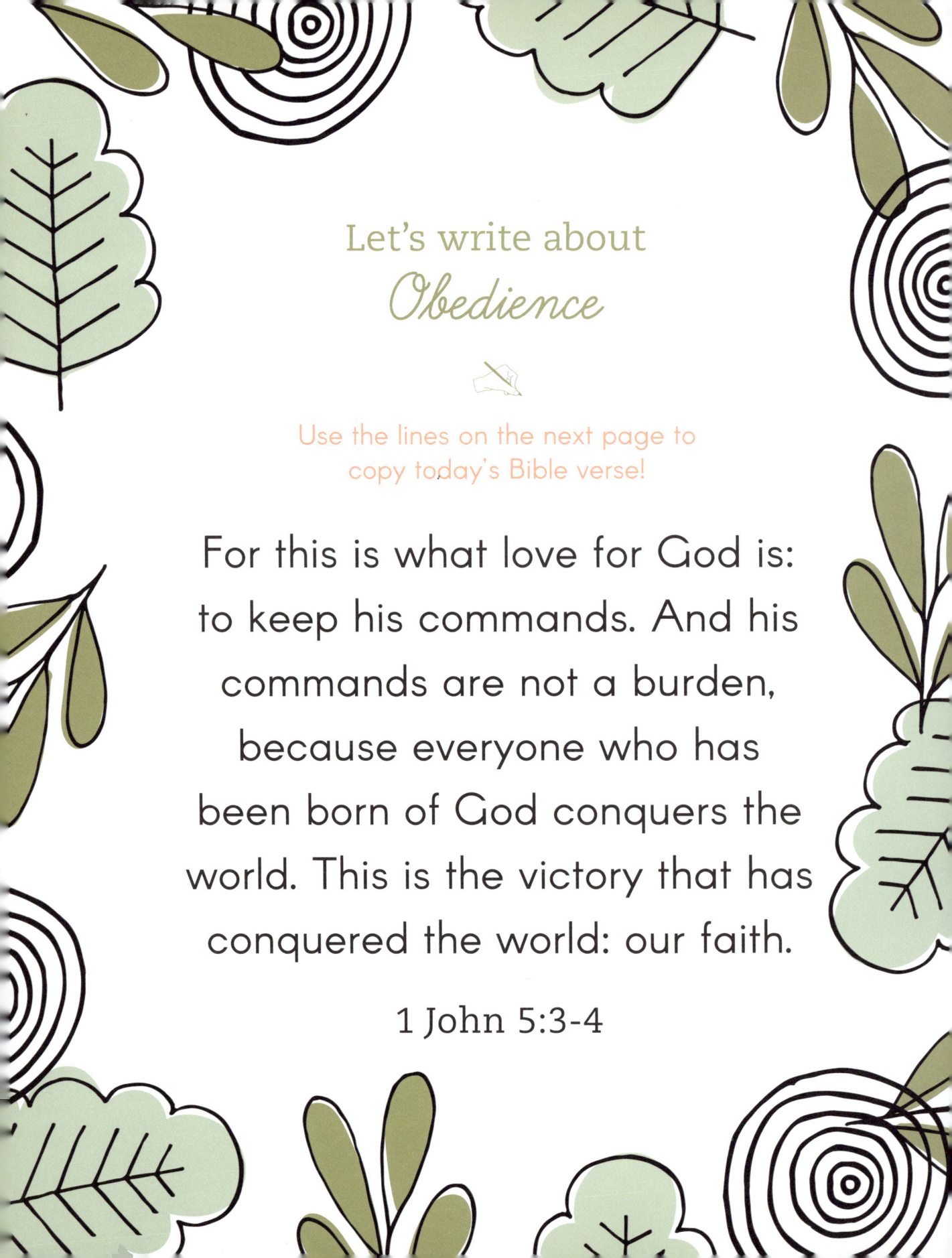

Use the lines on the next page to copy today's Bible verse!

For this is what love for God is: to keep his commands. And his commands are not a burden, because everyone who has been born of God conquers the world. This is the victory that has conquered the world: our faith.

1 John 5:3-4

First, write your name

Let's write about
Boldness

Use the lines on the next page to copy today's Bible verse!

For God has not given us a spirit of fear, but one of power, love, and sound judgment.

2 Timothy 1:7

First, write your name

Let's write about

Wisdom

Use the lines on the next page to copy today's Bible verse!

Guard your heart above all else, for it is the source of life.

Proverbs 4:23

First, write your name

Let's write about

Thankfulness

Use the lines on the next page to copy today's Bible verse!

Give thanks in everything; for this is God's will for you in Christ Jesus.

1 Thessalonians 5:18

First, write your name

Let's write about
Boldness

Use the lines on the next page to
copy today's Bible verse!

Haven't I commanded you:
be strong and courageous?
Do not be afraid or discouraged,
for the Lord your God is with
you wherever you go.

Joshua 1:9

First, write your name

Let's write about
Obedience

Use the lines on the next page to copy today's Bible verse!

Honor your father and your mother so that you may have a long life in the land that the Lord your God is giving you.

Exodus 20:12

First, write your name

Let's write about

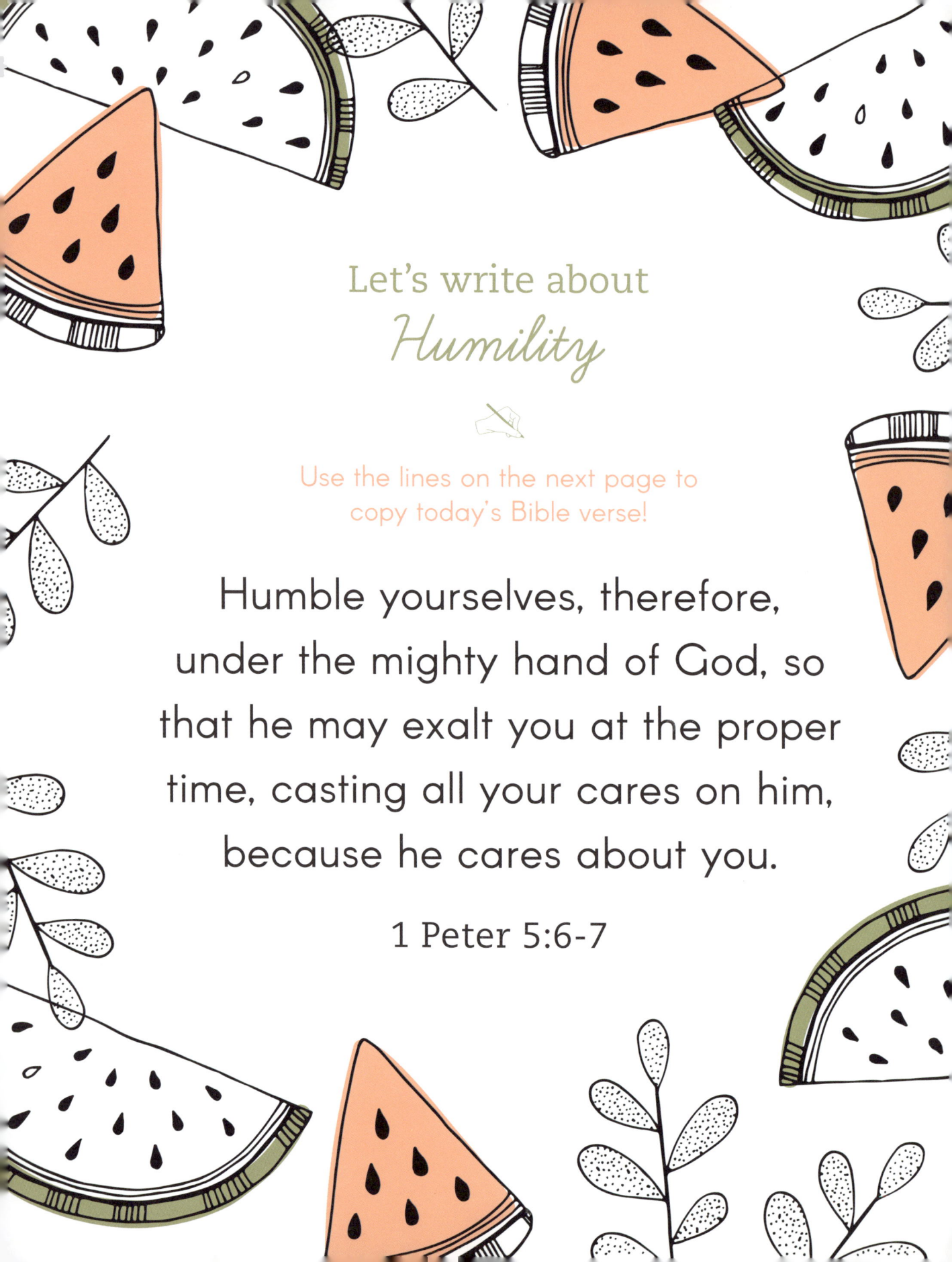

Humility

Use the lines on the next page to
copy today's Bible verse!

Humble yourselves, therefore, under the mighty hand of God, so that he may exalt you at the proper time, casting all your cares on him, because he cares about you.

1 Peter 5:6-7

First, write your name

Let's write about
Love

Use the lines on the next page to
copy today's Bible verse!

I give you a new command: Love one another. Just as I have loved you, you are also to love one another.

John 13:34

First, write your name

Let's write about
Faith

Use the lines on the next page to copy today's Bible verse!

I am sure of this, that he who started a good work in you will carry it on to completion until the day of Christ Jesus.

Philippians 1:6

First, write your name

Let's write about
Devotion

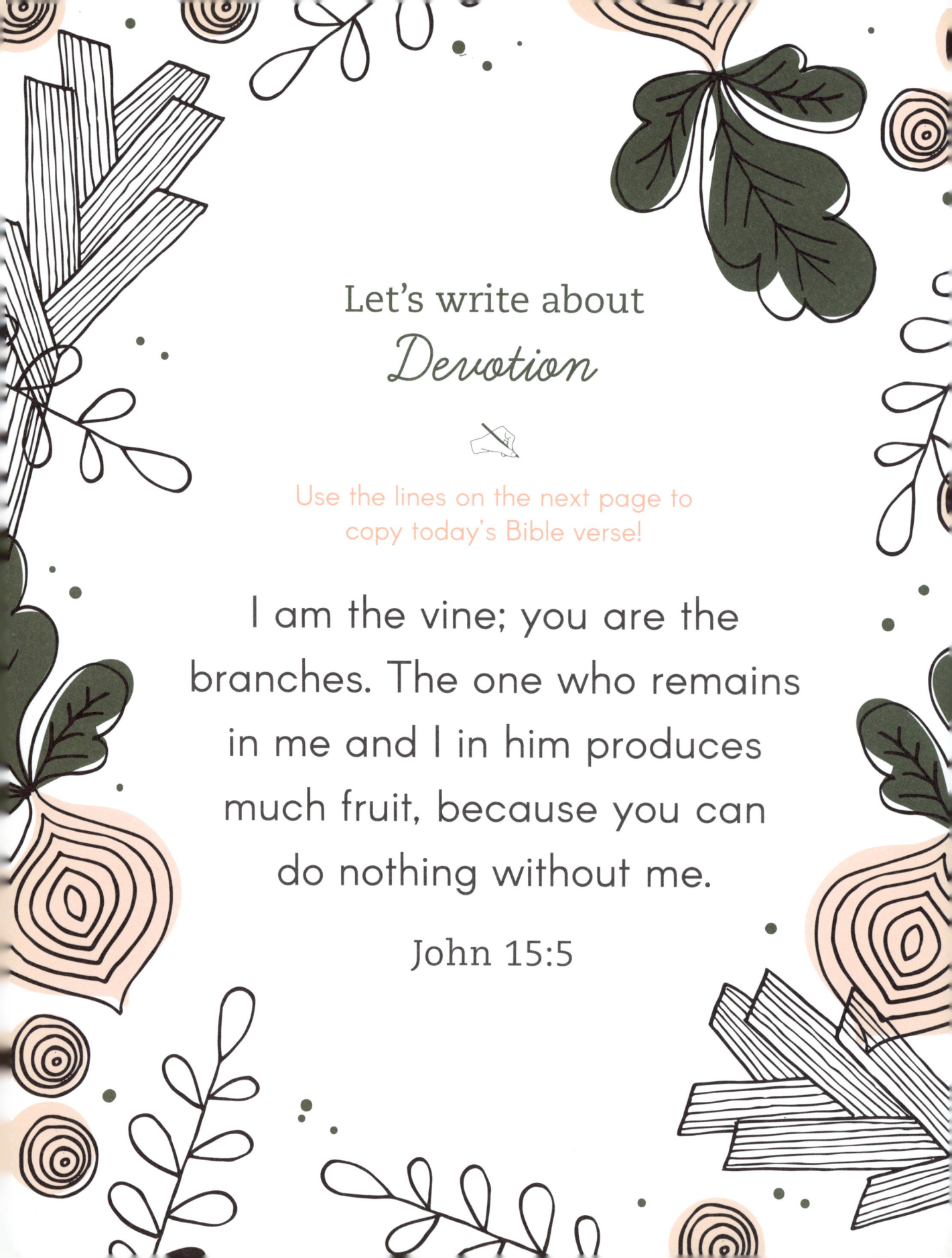

Use the lines on the next page to
copy today's Bible verse!

I am the vine; you are the branches. The one who remains in me and I in him produces much fruit, because you can do nothing without me.

John 15:5

First, write your name

Let's write about
Virtue

Use the lines on the next page to copy today's Bible verse!

In the same way, let your light shine before others, so that they may see your good works and give glory to your Father in heaven.

Matthew 5:16

First, write your name

Let's write about

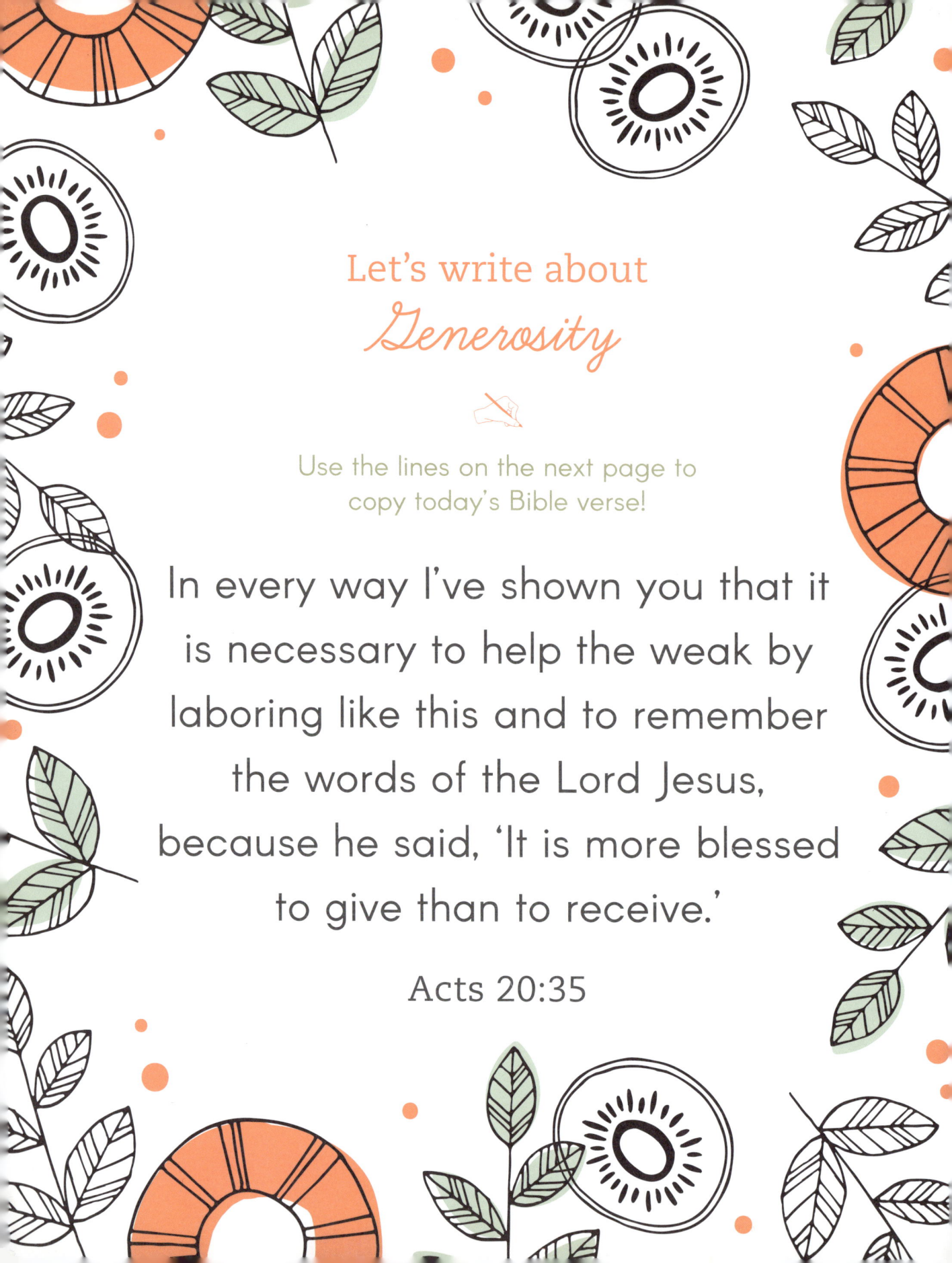

Generosity

Use the lines on the next page to copy today's Bible verse!

In every way I've shown you that it is necessary to help the weak by laboring like this and to remember the words of the Lord Jesus, because he said, 'It is more blessed to give than to receive.'

Acts 20:35

First, write your name

Let's write about

Hospitality

Use the lines on the next page to copy today's Bible verse!

Just as you want others to do for you, do the same for them

Luke 6:31

First, write your name

Let's write about

Contentment

Use the lines on the next page to copy today's Bible verse!

Keep your life free from the love of money. Be satisfied with what you have, for he himself has said, I will never leave you or abandon you.

Hebrews 13:5

First, write your name

Let's write about

Determination

Use the lines on the next page to copy today's Bible verse!

Let us not get tired of doing good, for we will reap at the proper time if we don't give up.

Galatians 6:9

First, write your name

Let's write about

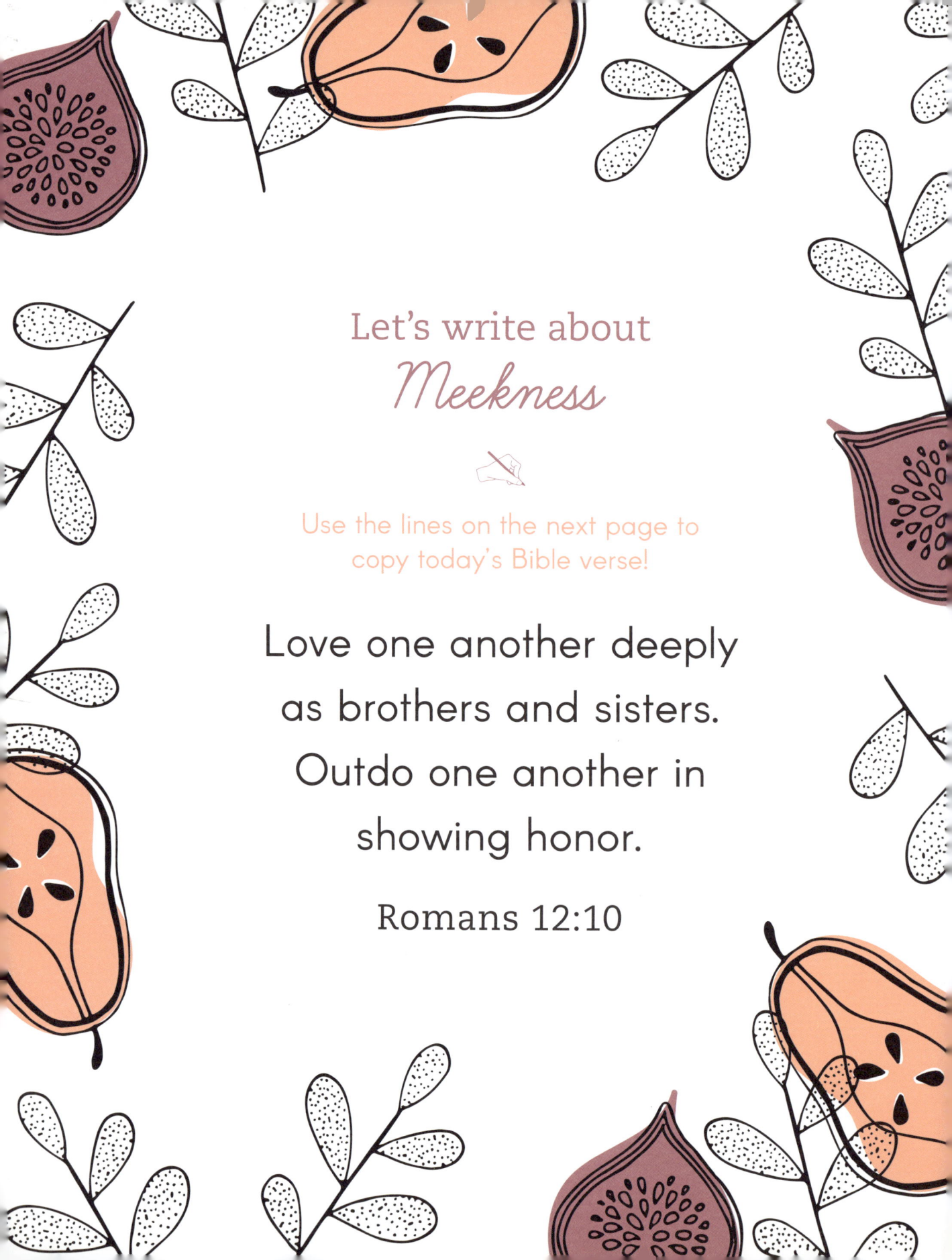

Meekness

Use the lines on the next page to copy today's Bible verse!

Love one another deeply as brothers and sisters. Outdo one another in showing honor.

Romans 12:10

First, write your name

Let's write about

Truthfulness

Use the lines on the next page to copy today's Bible verse!

Lying lips are detestable to the Lord, but faithful people are his delight.

Proverbs 12:22

First, write your name

Let's write about

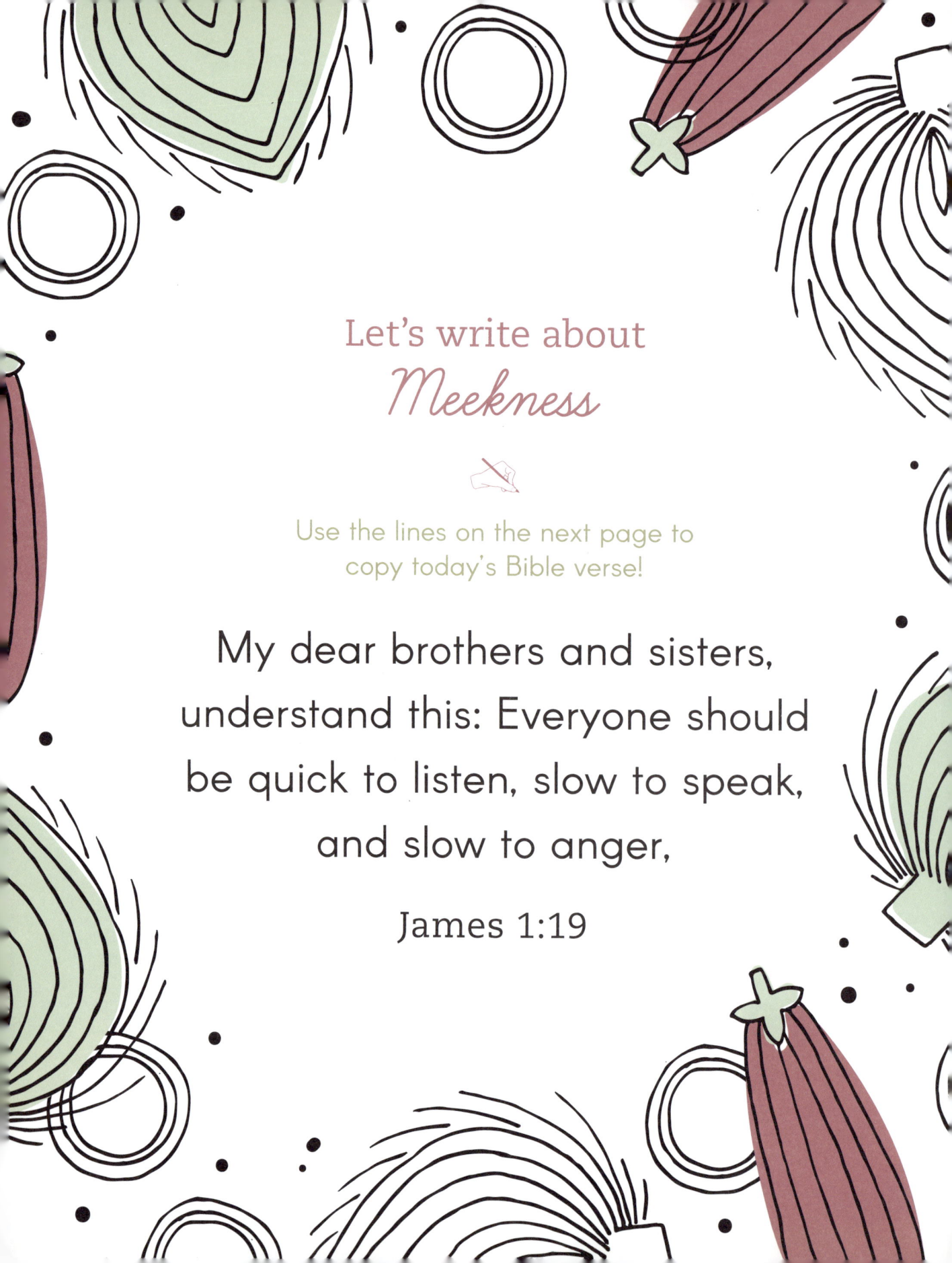

Meekness

Use the lines on the next page to copy today's Bible verse!

My dear brothers and sisters, understand this: Everyone should be quick to listen, slow to speak, and slow to anger,

James 1:19

First, write your name

Let's write about
Obedience

Use the lines on the next page to copy today's Bible verse!

My son, keep your father's command, and don't reject your mother's teaching. Always bind them to your heart; tie them around your neck.

Proverbs 6:20-21

First, write your name

Let's write about

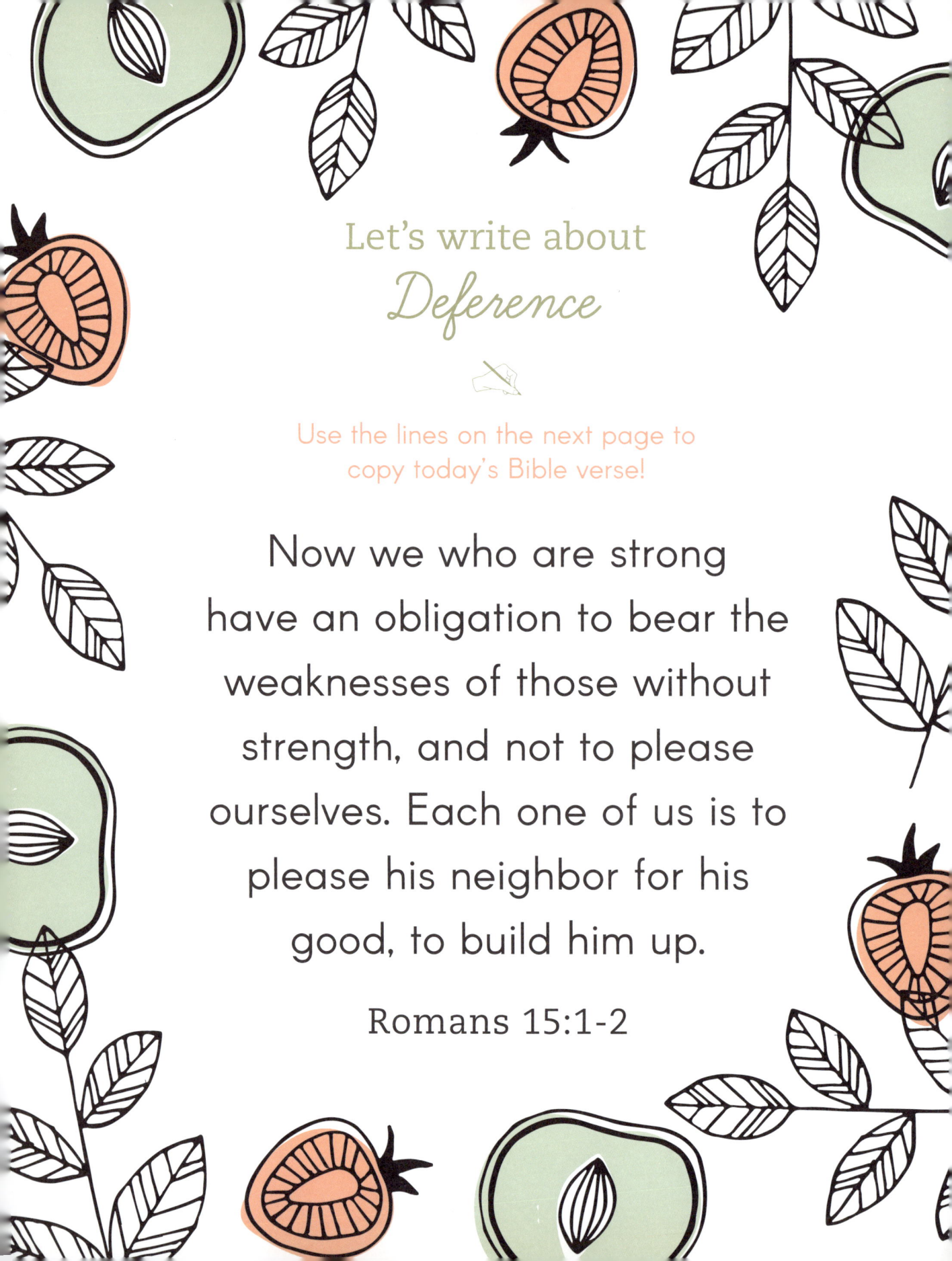

Deference

Use the lines on the next page to copy today's Bible verse!

Now we who are strong have an obligation to bear the weaknesses of those without strength, and not to please ourselves. Each one of us is to please his neighbor for his good, to build him up.

Romans 15:1-2

First, write your name

Let's write about
Meekness

Use the lines on the next page to copy today's Bible verse!

One who becomes stiff-necked, after many reprimands will be shattered instantly—beyond recovery. A fool gives full vent to his anger, but a wise person holds it in check.

Proverbs 29:1, 11

First, write your name

Let's write about
Boldness

Use the lines on the next page to copy today's Bible verse!

Put on the full armor of God so that you can stand against the schemes of the devil. For our struggle is not against flesh and blood, but against the rulers, against the authorities, against the cosmic powers of this darkness, against evil, spiritual forces in the heavens.

Ephesians 6:11-12

First, write your name

Let's write about
Thankfulness

Use the lines on the next page to
copy today's Bible verse!

Rejoice always, pray constantly, give thanks in everything; for this is God's will for you in Christ Jesus.

1 Thessalonians 5:16-18

First, write your name

Let's write about

Joyfulness

Use the lines on the next page to copy today's Bible verse!

Serve the Lord with gladness; come before him with joyful songs.

Psalm 100:2

First, write your name

Let's write about
Generosity

Use the lines on the next page to copy today's Bible verse!

Sell your possessions and give to the poor. Make money-bags for yourselves that won't grow old, an inexhaustible treasure in heaven, where no thief comes near and no moth destroys. For where your treasure is, there your heart will be also.

Luke 12:33-34

First, write your name

Let's write about
Devotion

Use the lines on the next page to
copy today's Bible verse!

So if you have been raised with Christ, seek the things above, where Christ is, seated at the right hand of God. Set your minds on things above, not on earthly things.

Colossians 3:1-2

First, write your name

Let's write about
Trust

Use the lines on the next page to copy today's Bible verse!

Trust in the Lord with all your heart, and do not rely on your own understanding; in all your ways know him, and he will make your paths straight.

Proverbs 3:5-6

First, write your name

Let's write about
Forgiveness

Use the lines on the next page to copy today's Bible verse!

Therefore, as God's chosen ones, holy and dearly loved, put on compassion, kindness, humility, gentleness, and patience, bearing with one another and forgiving one another if anyone has a grievance against another. Just as the Lord has forgiven you, so you are also to forgive.

Colossians 3:12-13

First, write your name

Let's write about
Devotion

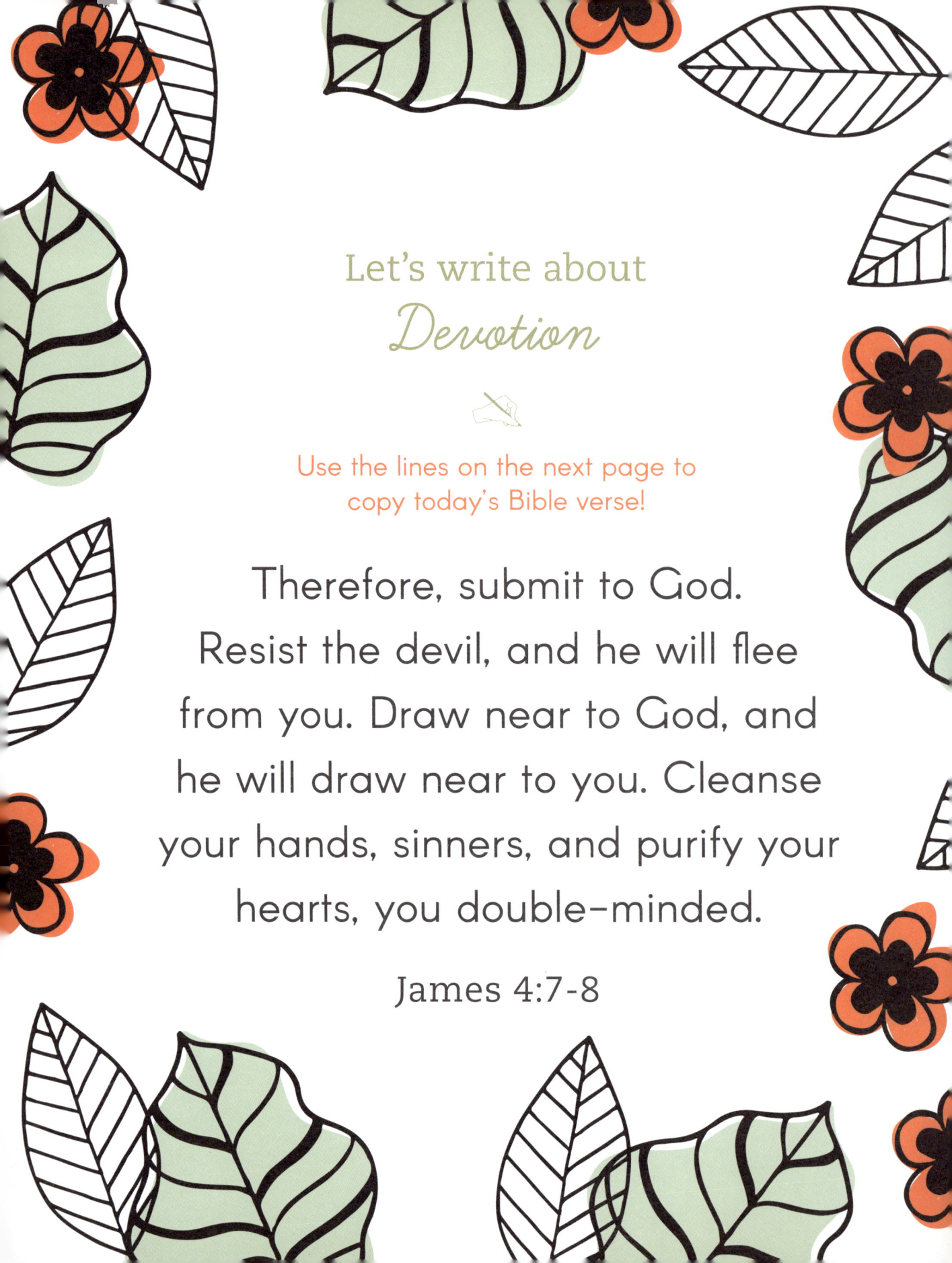

Use the lines on the next page to copy today's Bible verse!

Therefore, submit to God. Resist the devil, and he will flee from you. Draw near to God, and he will draw near to you. Cleanse your hands, sinners, and purify your hearts, you double-minded.

James 4:7-8

First, write your name

Let's write about

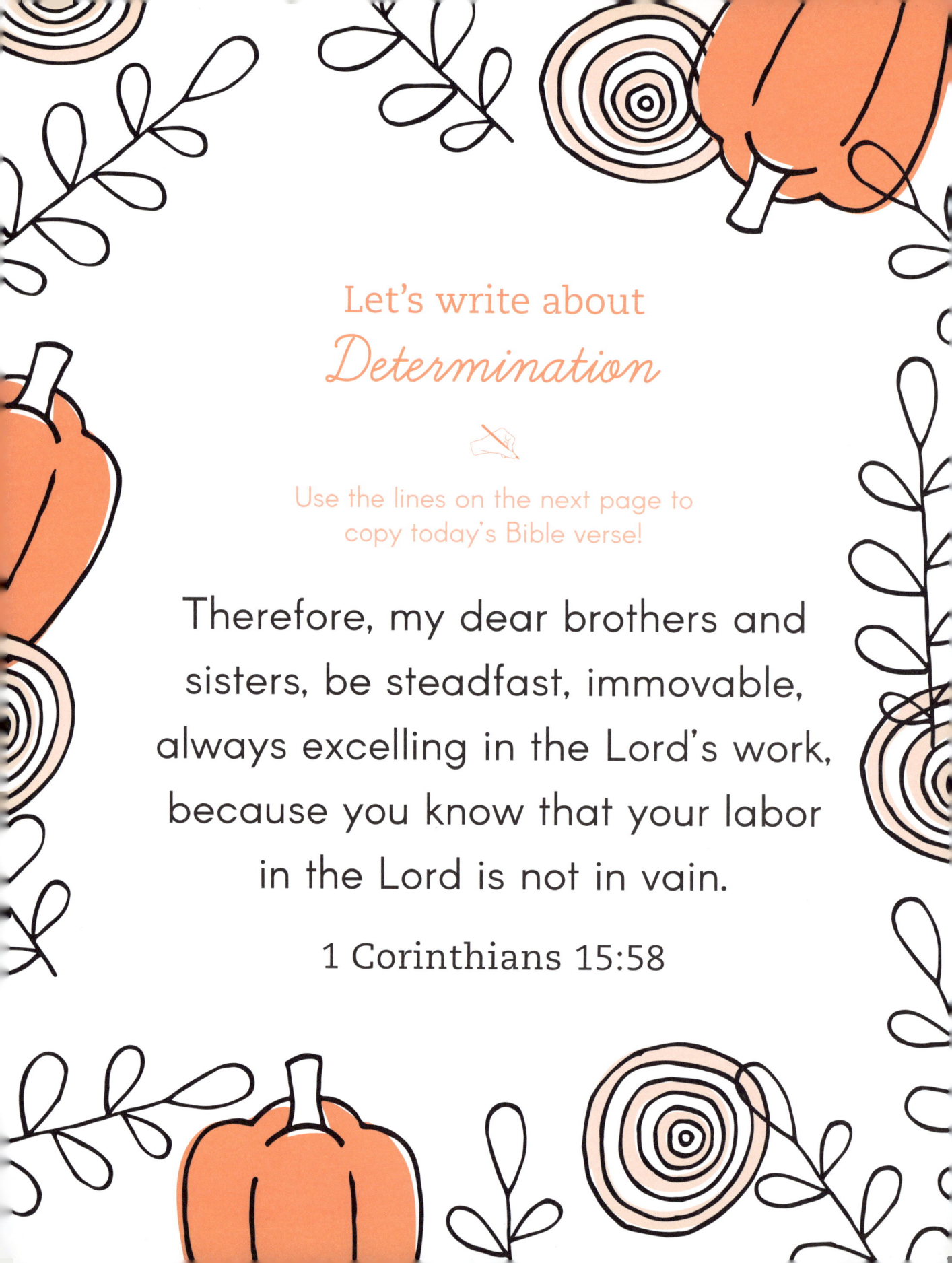

Determination

Use the lines on the next page to copy today's Bible verse!

Therefore, my dear brothers and sisters, be steadfast, immovable, always excelling in the Lord's work, because you know that your labor in the Lord is not in vain.

1 Corinthians 15:58

First, write your name

Let's write about

Creativity

Use the lines on the next page to
copy today's Bible verse!

Whatever you do, do it from the heart, as something done for the Lord and not for people.

Colossians 3:23

First, write your name

Let's write about

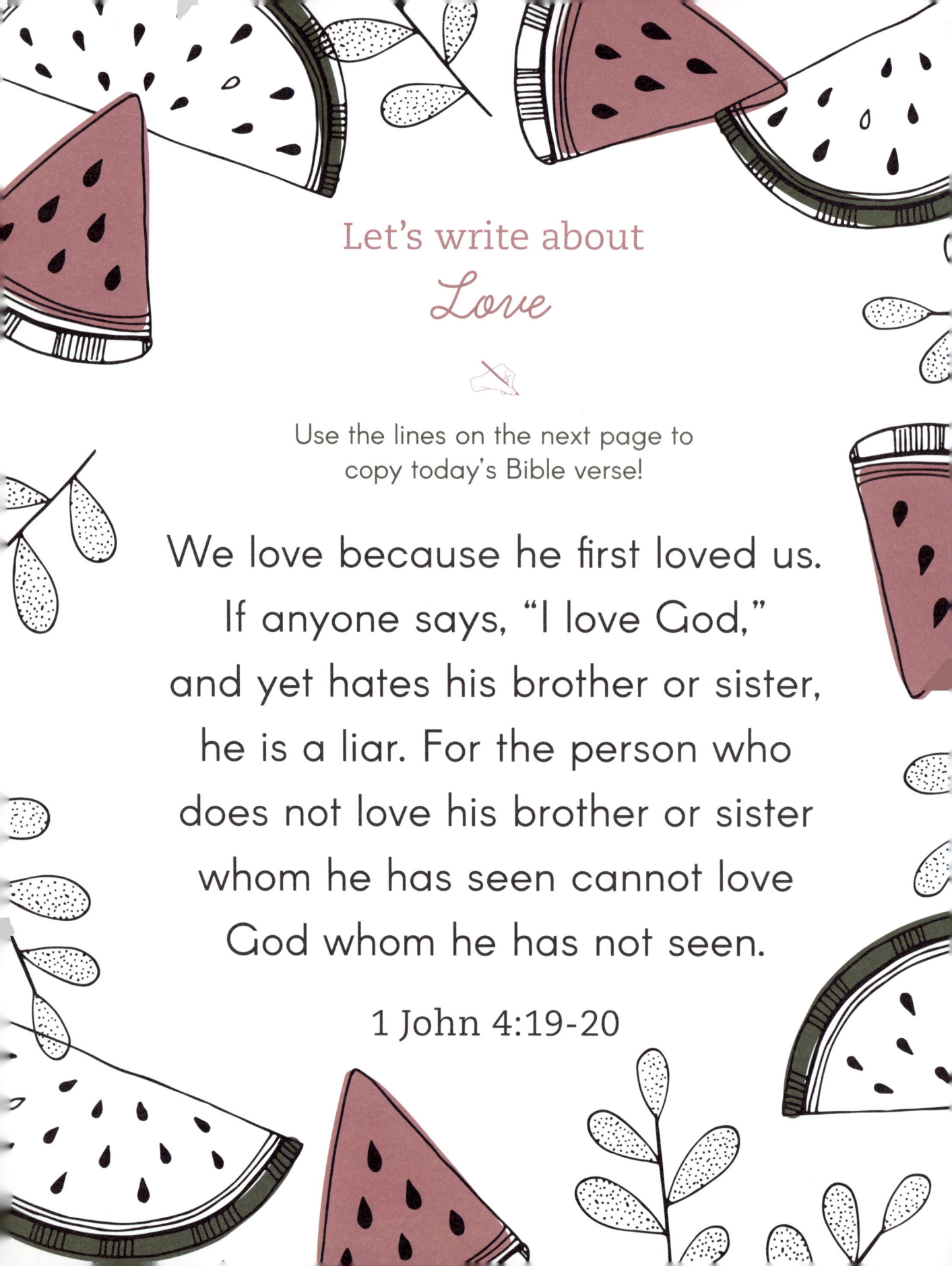

Love

Use the lines on the next page to
copy today's Bible verse!

We love because he first loved us. If anyone says, "I love God," and yet hates his brother or sister, he is a liar. For the person who does not love his brother or sister whom he has seen cannot love God whom he has not seen.

1 John 4:19-20

First, write your name

Let's write about

Joyfulness

Use the lines on the next page to copy today's Bible verse!

You reveal the path of life to me; in your presence is abundant joy; at your right hand are eternal pleasures.

Psalm 16:11

First, write your name

Let's write about
Trust

Use the lines on the next page to copy today's Bible verse!

Youths may become faint and weary, and young men stumble and fall, but those who trust in the Lord will renew their strength; they will soar on wings like eagles; they will run and not become weary, they will walk and not faint.

Isaiah 40:30-31

First, write your name

Thank You

for studying God's
Word with us!

CONNECT WITH US

@thedailygraceco
@kristinschmucker

CONTACT US

info@thedailygraceco.com

SHARE

#thedailygraceco
#lampandlight

WEBSITE

www.thedailygraceco.com